ADVENTURES WITH ATOMS AND MOLECULES

BOOK III

CHEMISTRY EXPERIMENTS FOR

YOUNG PEOPLE

ROBERT C. MEBANE

THOMAS R. RYBOLT

ENSLOW PUBLISHERS, INC.

Bloy St. & Ramsey Ave.   P.O. Box 38
Box 777   Aldershot
Hillside, N.J. 07205   Hants GU12 6BP
U.S.A.   U.K.

ACKNOWLEDGMENT

We wish to thank Paula Watson and Sandy Zitkus-Mebane for their helpful comments and corrections during the preparation of this book, and Greg Grant for his helpful suggestions regarding several of the experiments. Our thanks also to Ronald I. Perkins of Greenwich High School, Connecticut, and to A. M. Sarquis of Miami University, Ohio, for reviewing the manuscript.

DEDICATION

This book is dedicated to our wives Sandy and Ann.

Library of Congress Cataloging–in–Publication Data

Mebane, Robert C.
    Adventures with atoms and molecules.

    Includes indexes.
    Chemistry experiments for home or school demonstrate the properties and behavior of various kinds of atoms and molecules.
        1. Chemistry—Experiments—Juvenile literature.
2. Chemistry—Experiments. 3. Molecules—Experiments.
4. Experiments. I. Rybolt, Thomas R. II. Title.
QD38.M43 1985   540'.78   85-10177
ISBN 0-89490-120-6 (Book 1)
ISBN 0-89490-164-8 (Book 2)
ISBN 0-89490-254-7 (Book 3)

Printed in the United States of America

10 9 8 7 6 5 4 3 2

CONTENTS

FOREWORD

This book is the third in a series of books on chemistry experiments designed to show young people how interesting science can be. Continuing in the same format, the authors have developed another set of safe, interesting, "NEAT," "WOW" investigations that use common household materials. Each activity concludes with an explanation, along with ideas for "Other things to try."

Although the experiments are especially useful for students in upper elementary and middle schools, many are appropriate for both younger and older children. Lower primary teachers will find a number of activities to use in the classroom; junior high school teachers will find this a valuable resource for individual work by students. Even adults will be intrigued with answers to questions such as: Why does adding salt to a carbonated drink release bubbles of gas? How many food coloring molecules are necessary to color a glass of water?

All three volumes are a good source of ideas for science fair projects. In fact, both my niece and nephew have expanded upon a number of the activities in Books I and II for science fair projects. Melissa has studied the effect of soap on floating pepper (kindergarten), the production of carbon dioxide from vinegar and baking soda (first grade), and the effect of static electricity on soap bubbles (second grade). Craig has studied acid rain (third grade), and evidence for atoms and molecules (fifth grade).

The first two volumes have become known as "the green book" and "the blue book." This volume, no doubt, will be known as "the purple book."

The authors once again have provided parents and teachers with an ideal way to encourage young people to study chemistry using the kitchen as the laboratory.

Ronald I. Perkins
Assistant Director
Institute for Chemical Education
University of Wisconsin—Madison

INTRODUCTION

SCIENCE

Science is an adventure! Science is an adventure of asking questions and finding answers. Scientists are men and women who ask questions. Scientists answer questions by doing experiments and making observations. The results of their observations increase our knowledge and improve our understanding of the world around us.

Science is exciting because it never stops. There will always be new questions to ask. New questions lead to new experiments. New experiments lead to new knowledge and to new questions.

Experimentation is the heart of science. Experimentation lays the foundation upon which the basic principles of science are understood. You can gain a better feeling as to what science really is by doing science and experiencing science.

One way to share in the adventure of science is to do experiments. In our first two books, Adventures With Atoms and Molecules and Adventures With Atoms and Molecules, Book II, we presented sixty experiments and suggestions for over one hundred and twenty additional activities. Those books were a start, but there are many more experiments waiting to be done.

This book is a further collection of experiments that you can do at home or at school. These experiments will help you learn how to ask questions and find answers, and how to become a better observer. As you read about science and do experiments, you will learn more about yourself and your world. In asking questions and doing experiments, you will learn that observing and trying to understand the world around you is interesting and fun.

ATOMS, IONS, AND MOLECULES

One of the most important things that scientists have learned about our world is that EVERYTHING IS MADE OF ATOMS. Water, ice, air, sand, table salt, sugar, rocks, shoes, clothes, houses, bicycles, cars, leaves, trees, flowers, bees, ants, spiders, cows, horses, and people are all made of atoms.

Atoms are the basic building blocks of all things. There are 92 different kinds of natural atoms. A few additional atoms have been made by scientists in laboratories. Examples of natural atoms include: oxygen, hydrogen, carbon, nitrogen, mercury, gold, silver, sulfur, helium, chlorine, sodium, neon, nickel, copper, iron, silicon, phosphorus, aluminum, and calcium.

Atoms are found in all things. For example, a piece of aluminum foil is made of aluminum atoms. A diamond consists of carbon atoms. Sand is made of silicon and oxygen atoms. Table sugar is made of carbon, hydrogen, and oxygen atoms.

Molecules are combinations of tightly bound atoms. Water is a combination of hydrogen and oxygen atoms. Imagine you have a drop of water and you divide this drop into smaller and smaller drops. If you could continue to divide the drops enough times, you would eventually end up with a single water molecule. If you divide this water molecule any further, you would have two hydrogen atoms and one oxygen atom.

Scientists use models to represent molecules. Sometimes the models are made from small balls with the balls representing atoms. These models allow scientists to understand more about molecules.

Molecules that are made of only a few atoms are very small. Molecules are so small that you cannot see one even with the most powerful optical microscope. One drop of water contains two million quadrillion (2,000,000,000,000,000,000,000) molecules. If you took two million quadrillion pennies and stacked one on top of the other, you would have three hundred thousand (300,000) stacks of pennies. Each stack would reach from the Sun to Pluto. Pluto is the planet in our solar system that is the greatest distance from the sun.

If you could magnify one drop of water to the size of the earth, each water molecule would be about the size of an orange.

Polymers are giant molecules made by combining many smaller molecules. Some polymer molecules may contain several million atoms. Important natural polymers include natural rubber, starch, and DNA. Rubber bands and some automobile tires are made of natural rubber. Starch is found in many foods. DNA is the molecule of heredity. Some important polymers made by scientists are nylon, which is used in making fabrics, polyethylene, which is used to make plastic bags and plastic bottles, and polystyrene, which is used in making styrofoam cups and insulation.

Atoms are made of smaller particles. These smaller particles are electrons, protons, and neutrons. Electrons are negatively charged and they spin around the nucleus. The nucleus is the center of the atom and contains protons and neutrons. Protons are positively charged and neutrons have no charge.

Atoms and molecules that contain a charge are called ions. Ions have either a positive charge or a negative charge. Positive ions have more protons than electrons. Negative ions have more electrons than protons. Sodium chloride, which is the chemical name for table salt, is made of positive sodium ions and negative chlorine ions.

Atoms or ions combine in chemical reactions to make molecules, metal alloys, or salts. Chemical reactions can also involve changing one molecule into a different molecule or breaking one molecule down into smaller molecules, atoms, or ions.

ABOUT THE EXPERIMENTS IN THIS BOOK

In this book we present thirty experiments and suggestions for more than sixty additional activities. Many of the new experiments will show you how experimentation can be used to understand phenomena you encounter in your everyday life. Have you ever wondered why you should chew your food well, why sunscreens are used, why helium balloons become smaller more quickly than balloons filled with air, why you can skate on ice, why oil and grease are slippery, or how detergents help clean clothes? You will find out with the experiments in this book.

Each experiment is divided into five parts: 1) materials, 2) procedure, 3) observations, 4) discussion, and 5) other things to try. The materials are what you need to do the experiment. The procedure is what you do. The observations are what you see. The discussion explains what your observations tell you about atoms and molecules. The other things to try are additional questions and experiments which you can do to find out more about atoms and molecules.

This book is intended to be used and not just read. It is a guide toward doing, observing, and thinking science. The experimental activities described in this book are designed to give you an opportunity to experience science.

Do not worry about trying to understand everything about an experiment. You do not have to memorize words or meanings when you are first involved in science. You need to experience science first.

You do not have to do the experiments in the order they appear in the book. Each experimental activity has been written to stand completely alone. You will find that some experiments discuss the same ideas. It will help you to learn and understand these ideas to see them more than once.

Not every experiment you do will work the way you expect every time. Something may be different in the experiment when you do it. Repeat the experiment if it gives an unexpected result and think about what may be different.

Not all of the experiments in this book give immediate results. Some experiments in this book will take some time to see observable results. Some of the experiments in this book may take a shorter time than that suggested in the experiment. Some experiments may take a longer time than suggested. You must be patient when doing experiments.

The drawings in this book were done using a computer graphics system. They are not intended to be a photographic or artistic substitution for what you will do and observe. The purpose of the drawings is to direct your attention to one or two key features of what you may expect to observe when you do each experiment.

SAFETY NOTE

WHEN YOU DO THESE EXPERIMENTS MAKE SURE YOU

1) Obtain an adult's permission before you do these experiments and activities.

2) Get an adult to watch you when you do an experiment. They enjoy seeing experiments too.

3) Follow the specific directions given for each experiment.

4) Clean up after each experiment.

NOTE TO TEACHERS, PARENTS, AND OTHER ADULTS

All of us are born with a natural curiosity regarding the world around us. This intrinsic interest in nature is the motivation for most scientific activity. To avoid a dulling of this interest as children grow older, it is necessary to provide experiences for young people which show the connection of science to everyday life and the world around us.

Science is not merely a collection of facts but a way of thinking. Our series of books, *Adventures With Atoms and Molecules*, is a tool to help children and young people become actively involved in the process of science. Explanations for each experimental activity are provided for completeness, but the experience of the activity is more important than the explanation. The experience can last a lifetime, and understanding can develop with time.

As teachers, parents, and other adults, you can play a key role in maintaining and encouraging a young person's interest in science. As you do experiments with a young person, you may find your own curiosity being expanded.

Remember, science is for everyone!

The adventure continues . . .

CAN AIR BE WEIGHED?

Materials

A meter stick or yardstick   Two paper clips

Three pieces of string   Two large balloons

It is easier to do this experiment with two large balloons. Try to find balloons that will inflate to twelve inches or more across. If you cannot find two large balloons, you can use six smaller balloons.

Procedure

A balance is used to weigh things. To make a balance like the one shown, tie a paper clip to each end of a meter stick using string. Tie a piece of string to the middle of the meter stick. Attach a large, deflated balloon onto each paper clip. (If you are using small balloons, attach three deflated balloons to each paper clip.)

Have a friend hold the string that is tied to the middle of the meter stick. Move this string along the meter stick until you get the balloons balanced at the same height from the floor. Have your friend holding the string tied to the middle of the meter stick also hold one end of the meter stick. Remove the large balloon attached to this end of the balance. Inflate the balloon and tie it off. (If you are using small balloons, remove and inflate the three balloons attached to one end of the meter stick.) Attach the inflated balloon to the end of the meter stick your friend is holding. Ask your friend to let go of the end of the meter stick. Observe what happens.

Observations

Which balloon moves down? Does the deflated balloon or the inflated balloon move down?

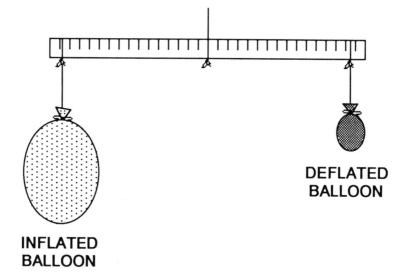

DEFLATED BALLOON

INFLATED BALLOON

Discussion

Air is a mixture of gases that surrounds the earth and is important to living things. Air is mostly made of nitrogen and oxygen molecules. There are approximately seventy-eight nitrogen molecules and twenty-one oxygen molecules out of every one hundred air molecules. Air also contains some argon, carbon dioxide, and water.

All molecules have weight on earth because gravity pulls on molecules. A balance is used to compare the weights of objects. In this experiment you make a balance with a meter stick and some string. When two identical objects with the same weight are attached to your balance, they should be at the same height from the floor. This is why you move the string along the meter stick until the two deflated balloons are balanced at the same height from the floor.

When you inflated one of the balloons with air, you added the weight of air molecules to the balloon. This is why the balloon filled with air should move lower than the balloon that is not inflated.

Gas molecules are very far apart. Most of the space in a gas is empty. Large balloons are used in this experiment so that enough air molecules are in the inflated balloon to show the difference in weight between an inflated balloon and a deflated balloon.

Other things to try

Try inflating the large balloon with a bicycle pump or a foot pump. Does the inflated balloon still move lower when it is attached to the balance?

Repeat the above experiment using two large balloons on each end of the meter stick. Does the end containing two inflated balloons move closer to the floor than when you used one balloon on each end?

2 IS COLD AIR HEAVIER THAN WARM AIR?

Materials

A refrigerator freezer

Procedure

Open the freezer door of the refrigerator. Place your hand below the freezer compartment. Do you feel cold air falling on your hand? Place your hand above the freezer compartment. Do you feel cold air? MAKE SURE TO CLOSE THE FREEZER DOOR. DO NOT LEAVE THE FREEZER DOOR OPEN FOR MORE THAN A MINUTE.

Observations

Do you feel cold air falling on your hand when your hand is below the freezer compartment? Do you feel cold air on your hand when your hand is above the freezer compartment?

Discussion

Air is a mixture of gases. Air is made mostly of nitrogen and oxygen molecules. Gas molecules are far apart. Most of the space between gas molecules is empty.

Density is a term used to compare the heaviness of the same volume of different substances. When molecules move closer together, the collection of molecules becomes more dense.

Gas molecules move closer together when they get colder. Air molecules in a freezer are colder than the air molecules in a warm room. Cold air in the freezer is heavier, or more dense, than the air in the warm room because the air molecules in the freezer are closer together. You should feel air falling on your hand when your hand is below the freezer compartment because the heavier, cold air falls.

Other things to try

Open the freezer door. Hold a piece of tissue paper below the freezer door. Does the piece of tissue paper move back and forth? Hold a piece of tissue paper above the freezer door. Does the piece of tissue paper move back and forth as much as when it is below the freezer door? Make sure to close the freezer door.

3 CAN CARBON DIOXIDE GAS MAKE RAISINS FLOAT IN WATER?

Materials

A clear glass

An unopened can or bottle of Sprite

Raisins

Procedure

Set the glass on a table. Open the Sprite. Fill the glass with Sprite. Drop five raisins in the glass of Sprite. Watch the raisins.

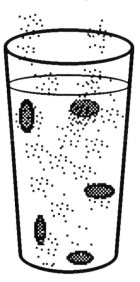

RAISINS
IN A GLASS
OF SPRITE

Observations

Do you see bubbles when the Sprite is opened and poured into the glass? Do the raisins sink to the bottom of the glass? Do bubbles collect on the surface of the raisins? Do the raisins with bubbles attached rise to the top of the glass? Do you see raisins rising and sinking in the glass?

Discussion

Sprite is a carbonated drink. Carbonated drinks contain carbon dioxide molecules. The bubbles you see in a Sprite are collections of carbon dioxide gas molecules. Sprite also contains sugar water and flavorings.

Density is the measure of the weight of a certain volume of a substance. Different solids and liquids have different densities. Sprite is a liquid. A raisin is a solid. If a solid is more dense than a liquid it will sink. If a solid is less dense than a liquid it will float. Carbon dioxide is a gas. Gases are less dense than liquids and solids. Bubbles of carbon dioxide float to the top of a liquid because they are less dense.

When the raisins are first added to the Sprite, they usually sink. The raisins are more dense than the liquid. Bubbles of carbon dioxide collect on the wrinkled surface of each raisin. The combination of gas bubbles and raisin has a lower density than water. The bubbles lower the density of the raisin, and it floats to the top of the glass of Sprite.

When a raisin reaches the top of the liquid, the bubbles of carbon dioxide break apart. The carbon dioxide gas leaves the raisins and moves out into the air. Without the carbon dioxide bubbles, the raisin is more dense than the liquid and it sinks.

Submarines under the ocean are able to rise to the surface or sink to the bottom by changing their density. When water is pumped into chambers in the submarine, the submarine sinks. When water is pumped out and the chambers are filled with air from tanks of compressed air, the submarine rises. By controlling the density of the submarine, the crew is able to control the exact depth of the submarine under the ocean.

Other things to try

Continue to watch the raisins "dance" as they rise and sink in the glass. After a while do all the raisins stop moving and settle to the bottom of the glass? After most of the carbon dioxide escapes from the Sprite, there are no more bubbles to attach to the raisins, and they will probably sink.

Repeat this experiment with two glasses of Sprite. Put two raisins in one glass and put twenty or more raisins in the other glass. Watch the raisins in both glasses and see if the raisins in one glass quit "dancing" first.

Would this experiment work with Sprite that has been left opened for several days? Try it and see. Try repeating this experiment with other carbonated drinks.

IS A DIET CARBONATED DRINK MORE DENSE OR LESS DENSE THAN A NONDIET CARBONATED DRINK? **4**

Materials

Kitchen sink or large pail

An unopened diet carbonated drink in an aluminum can (such as Diet Coke)

An unopened nondiet carbonated drink in an aluminum can (such as regular Coke)

An opened, empty drink can made of aluminum.

Procedure

Fill the sink with warm water. The depth of water in the sink must be greater than the height of a drink can. Use a large pail if your sink is not large enough. Place the unopened can of a diet carbonated drink in the water. Place the unopened can of a nondiet carbonated drink in the water. Observe what happens.

Most diet carbonated drinks will float. Most nondiet carbonated drinks will sink. If the diet carbonated drink does not float, try another one. If the nondiet carbonated drink floats, try another one.

Rinse out an empty drink can with water. Fill the can with water. Place the can in the sink of water. Make sure the can is completely full of water. Observe what happens.

Observations

Does the diet carbonated drink sink or float? Does the nondiet carbonated drink sink or float? Does the empty drink can filled with water sink or float?

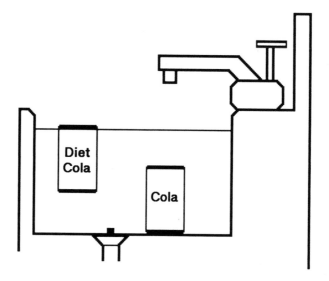

Discussion

In this experiment the diet carbonated drink should float and the nondiet carbonated drink should sink. A nondiet carbonated drink is heavier, or more dense, than a diet carbonated drink. Substances of the same volume that are heavier than other substances are more dense than the other substances.

Today most drink cans are made of aluminum metal. Aluminum metal is more dense than water. This is why the empty drink can filled with water should sink when it is placed in the water. Why then does the nondiet drink sink and the diet drink float in water since they are both in aluminum cans?

Both drinks contain carbonated water. Carbonated water has carbon dioxide molecules in it. Most of the carbon dioxide molecules are dissolved in the liquid part of the drink which is mostly water. There are some carbon dioxide molecules in the space between the liquid and the top of the can. These carbon dioxide molecules are a gas.

Carbon dioxide gas is less dense than water.

The carbon dioxide gas trapped in the top of the can makes the filled diet drink can less dense than water. This is why the diet carbonated drink floats in water. The carbon dioxide gas in the nondiet carbonated drink would also make the nondiet drink less dense for water, but the sweetener in the nondiet drink makes the drink more dense than water.

A nondiet carbonated drink is usually sweetened with corn sugar and table sugar. Glucose is the chemical name for corn sugar and sucrose is the chemical name for table sugar. Diet carbonated drinks are usually sweetened with an artificial sweetener like Nutrasweet or saccharin. When corn sugar and sucrose dissolve in water, the solution becomes more dense than water. There is enough corn sugar and sucrose dissolved in a nondiet carbonated drink to make the drink more dense than water. This is why the nondiet drink sinks in water. There is not enough artificial sweetener in a diet carbonated drink to make the drink much more dense than water. Artificial sweeteners are hundreds of times more sweet than corn sugar and sucrose, so much less has to be used to sweeten a drink.

Generally, a food label lists what is in the food starting with the most abundant ingredient and going to the least abundant ingredient. Compare the labels of a diet and nondiet drinks. Can you tell that there is more sugar (corn syrup and sucrose) in a non-diet drink than there is artificial sweetener in a diet drink?

Other things to try

Try other diet and nondiet carbonated drinks in a can. Do all the diet carbonated drinks float? Do all the nondiet carbonated drinks sink? Do you understand why?

Try diet and nondiet carbonated drinks bottled in plastic bottles. Do you get the same results as the drinks in cans?

Try diet and nondiet carbonated drinks bottled in glass bottles. Do you get the same results as the carbonated drinks bottled in plastic or in cans? Both the diet and nondiet carbonated drinks bottled in glass should sink. The glass makes the drinks more dense than water.

If you have a kitchen balance, try weighing a canned diet and nondiet carbonated drink. Is there any difference in the weights?

DOES ADDING SALT TO A CARBONATED DRINK CAUSE GAS TO BE RELEASED? **5**

Materials

A clear carbonated drink such as Sprite or 7-Up

A glass

A salt shaker

Procedure

Fill a glass three-fourths full with a clear carbonated drink such as Sprite or 7-Up. Sprinkle a few crystals of salt from a salt shaker into the glass. Observe what happens.

CARBONATED DRINKS

WITH SALT ADDED   WITHOUT SALT ADDED

Observations

Do you see gas bubbles rising in the carbonated drink before you add salt to the drink? Do you see more gas bubbles rising in the drink when you sprinkle a few crystals of salt in the glass? Are gas bubbles forming on the salt crystals as the salt crystals drop to the bottom of the glass?

Discussion

A carbonated drink contains carbon dioxide molecules dissolved in water. Some of the carbon dioxide molecules become a gas when you open a carbonated drink. The bubbles you see when you open a carbonated drink are carbon dioxide gas.

When salt is added to a carbonated drink, more carbonated gas bubbles should be seen in the glass. Salt causes more carbon dioxide molecules to escape as a gas. The carbon dioxide molecules in the water gather on the surfaces of the salt crystals. When enough carbon dioxide molecules gather together on the surface of a salt crystal, they form a gas bubble and leave the liquid. When a surface causes molecules to gather together, the process is called nucleation.

Scientists sometimes use nucleation to make rain. They do this by releasing small particles in clouds as they fly through the clouds in an airplane. Water molecules in the clouds gather on the surfaces of the small particles. When enough water molecules gather on the small particles, water droplets form and fall to earth as rain.

Other things to try

Place a glass containing a clear carbonated drink in the sink. Add a teaspoon of salt to the glass. Are more gas bubbles released when a teaspoon of salt is added to the drink than when a few crystals of salt are added?

Repeat this experiment using table sugar. Do you get similar results? Try using baking soda.

Fill a glass three-fourths full with a clear carbonated drink. Stir the drink with a spoon. Do you see more gas bubbles form when you stir the drink?

CAN YOU SEE THROUGH A

6

BALLOON WHEN IT IS INFLATED?

Materials

A balloon   A lamp or window

Procedure

Hold a deflated balloon towards a brightly lit window or a lamp. Try to look through the balloon. Inflate the balloon by blowing into the balloon. Hold it closed with your fingers. Hold the balloon toward the brightly lit window or a lamp. Try to look through the balloon.

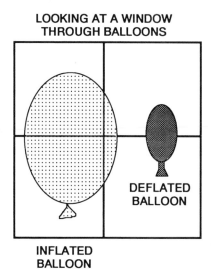

LOOKING AT A WINDOW
THROUGH BALLOONS

DEFLATED
BALLOON

INFLATED
BALLOON

Observations

Can you see through the deflated balloon? Can you see through the balloon when it is inflated?

Discussion

A balloon is made of rubber molecules. Balloons also contain some dye molecules that give the balloon its color. Rubber is a special kind of molecule called a polymer. Polymers are very large molecules and are made by joining together smaller molecules into long chains. A polymer is like a bicycle chain because a bicycle chain is made of many small links joined together.

When a balloon is deflated, the large rubber molecules coil around each other in layers like cooked spaghetti in a bowl. The dye molecules in the balloon are trapped in the layers of coiled rubber molecules. Light cannot pass through the layers of coiled rubber molecules and the trapped dye molecules. This is why you should not be able to see through the balloon when it is deflated.

When the balloon is inflated, the large, coiled rubber molecules are stretched. The coiled rubber molecules are straightened when they are stretched. The more the balloon is inflated, the more the rubber molecules are stretched and the straighter the rubber molecules become. When the rubber molecules in the balloon are stretched, the layer of rubber molecules in the wall of the balloon becomes thinner. The trapped dye molecules also move farther apart as the rubber molecules are stretched. Light can pass through the balloon when it is inflated because the layer of rubber molecules is thinner and the dye molecules are farther apart. This is why you should be able to see through the balloon when it is inflated.

Other things to try

Inflate a balloon and hold it tightly closed with your fingers. Look through the inflated balloon toward a brightly lit window or lamp. Gently move your fingers to let some air out of the balloon. Does the brightly lit window or lamp you see through the balloon get darker as you let air out of the balloon? Is there still some air in the balloon when you can no longer see the brightly lit window or lamp through the balloon?

Try different colored balloons. Do you get similar results?

DOES HELIUM PASS THROUGH A BALLOON FASTER THAN AIR?

7

Materials

A balloon filled with helium

An empty balloon of the same type

Procedure

Next time you get a balloon filled with helium you can do this experiment. You may find a helium balloon at a carnival or fair or balloon shop. Make sure that it is a balloon that will stretch. Stretchy balloons are made of rubber or latex and will work more quickly for this experiment. Nonstretchy balloons are made of mylar and hold gases for a long time.

Get another balloon that is similar to your helium-filled balloon. Blow up the empty balloon with air to the same size as the helium balloon. Tie the balloon closed with a strong knot. Make sure the helium balloon is closed with the same type of knot.

Set the balloons in a place where they can stay for several days. Compare the sizes of the balloons each day for at least four days.

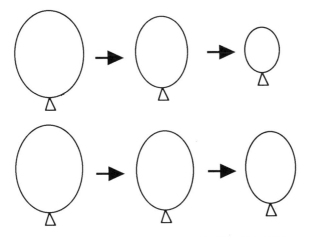

CHANGE WITH TIME FOR HELIUM AND AIR

Observations

Are the two balloons the same size at the start of your experiment? Do the sizes of the balloons change from day to day? Does one of the balloons get smaller while the other one stays the same?

Discussion

The balloon filled with air contains mostly nitrogen and oxygen molecules. Each nitrogen molecule is made of two nitrogen atoms. Each oxygen molecule is made of two oxygen atoms. Nitrogen and oxygen molecules are about the same size.

Helium gas consists of separate helium atoms. Helium atoms do not combine with other atoms to form molecules. Nitrogen and oxygen molecules in air are larger and heavier than helium atoms.

There is enough space between the rubber molecules in the balloon to let the helium atoms pass through the balloon. Air molecules can also pass through the balloon. However, the helium atoms can pass through the balloon much faster than the air molecules because the helium atoms are smaller than the air molecules.

Other things to try

Repeat this experiment with another helium-filled balloon. Wrap a string around the middle of the balloon to measure the balloon's size. Use a ruler to measure the length of string required to just reach around the balloon. Check the size of the balloon each day for four days. Write down the length of string that reaches around the balloon each day. Do these measurements show that the helium balloon is getting smaller?

Make a series of measurements of size for a balloon filled with air as described above. How do these sizes compare to the helium balloon sizes?

Can you explain why a helium balloon stops floating in air after several days?

CAN AIR PRESSURE BE STRONGER THAN GRAVITY?

8

Materials

A rubber plumber's plunger

A smooth board

Procedure

Set the smooth board flat on the floor. Hold the wooden handle of the plunger. Push the rubber plunger against the smooth board. Push hard enough to flatten the curved surface of the rubber plunger. Now release the wooden handle. Lift the board and hold the board sideways.

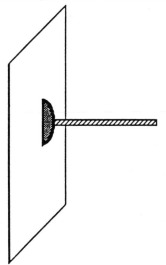

Observations

When you release the handle, does the plunger fall to the floor? Does the plunger stay pressed against the board?

Discussion

Gravity is the force that pulls objects toward the center of the earth. Normally if you release an object, it falls to the ground. The plunger does not fall because it is held against the board by air pressure.

Near the earth the air in our atmosphere pushes on every square inch of surface with a weight of about fifteen pounds. We don't feel this weight because it is all around us. The push due to air is called air pressure.

When you push the rubber plunger against a surface, air is pushed out of the plunger and a vacuum is created. A vacuum is the absence of air. When you release the plunger, the air in the room continues to push the plunger against the surface. But now there is less air underneath the rubber plunger. The extra air pressure on the outside of the plunger holds it against the board. The air pressure is stronger than gravity.

The plunger will not fall unless you push on the side of the rubber to let air underneath the plunger. If you wait a while, air may gradually leak underneath the plunger, and the plunger will fall.

If you use a rough surface, air will quickly go into the plunger, and it will not stay pressed against the surface.

In 1654, Otto von Guericke, a German engineer and city mayor, pumped all the air out of two large copper spheres that were touching each other. By removing the air between the spheres, a vacuum was created. It took two teams of eight horses to pull the copper spheres apart. This experiment demonstrated the strength of air pressure pushing against a vacuum.

Other things to try

Push the plunger down against the bottom of a bathtub or smooth wooden floor. Hold the wooden handle and try to lift the plunger. Can you lift it? Does it feel like something is holding the plunger down?

Take two plungers that are the same size and push them together. Push them hard enough to squeeze the air out between them. Now try to pull them apart. Can you do it?

DOES AIR PRESSURE INCREASE AS AIR IS WARMED?

9

Materials

A tire pressure gauge   An automobile

Procedure

ASK AN ADULT TO HELP YOU WITH THIS EXPERIMENT. This experiment should be done when you are going to take a trip in an automobile. The automobile must have been parked for at least two hours so the tires will not be hot when you start.

Ask an adult to help you use a tire gauge to measure the pressure of the air inside an automobile tire. Touch the automobile tire to feel the temperature. Now go for a ride in the automobile. The automobile should be driven twenty minutes or longer at highway speeds. After the car stops, use the tire gauge to check the air pressure of the same tire. Touch the tire.

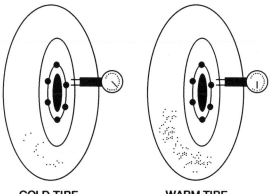

COLD TIRE   WARM TIRE

Observations

What is the tire pressure before the trip? What is the tire pressure after the trip? When you touch the tire, does it feel warmer than before the car was driven?

Discussion

Air is mostly made of molecules of nitrogen and oxygen. These air

31

molecules are in constant motion inside an automobile tire. The push of the molecules on the inside of the tire keeps the tire from collapsing.

The push due to the motion of molecules is called pressure. A tire gauge compares the air pressure in the tire to the pressure of the atmosphere. A typical tire pressure is about 30 pounds per square inch. This means that the air inside the tire is pushing out on each square inch of the tire with a pressure 30 pounds greater than the pressure in the atmosphere. The pressure in the atmosphere is around 14 pounds per square inch.

When air gets colder, the gas molecules in air (mostly nitrogen and oxygen) move slower. When air gets warmer, the molecules in air move faster. When the molecules in air move faster, they bounce against the inside wall of a tire more often and with more energy. When molecules in air bounce faster and with more energy, the air pressure increases.

As a car is driven, the tires roll across the road to push the car forward. The rubbing of the tires on the road causes the tires to get warmer. This makes the air inside the tire warmer and increases the tire pressure. It is not the speed of the tire turning that makes the molecules move faster, but the fact that the tire gets warmer.

Car owners are usually instructed to check the tire pressure when the tire is cold. The cold tire pressure is the pressure before the car is driven. After the car is driven, the tire will be warmer and the air pressure higher.

Other things to try

Measure the tire pressure immediately after you have finished a trip in the car. Then check the pressure again after the car has set for several hours. Did the pressure increase or decrease as the tires cooled?

During the change from summer to winter, it is common to add air to automobile tires to keep the tires' pressures from dropping. During the change from winter to summer, it is sometimes necessary to release air from tires to keep the pressures from being too high. Can you explain why the tire pressure changes during the year?

DO MOLECULES OF WATER TAKE UP   **10**
LESS SPACE AS A LIQUID OR A GAS?

Materials

An empty plastic milk jug with cap   A pot holder

A microwave oven   Water

A measuring cup

Procedure

ASK AN ADULT TO HELP YOU WITH THIS EXPERIMENT.
NEVER PUT METAL INTO A MICROWAVE OVEN! MAKE SURE THE
PLASTIC JUG HAS NO METAL AROUND THE TOP. ONLY DO THIS
EXPERIMENT WITH A PLASTIC JUG. NEVER USE GLASS. NEVER
HEAT A JUG THAT IS CAPPED.

Pour one-half cup of water into an empty gallon or half-gallon
plastic jug. Place the jug on its side in the microwave oven. Close the
microwave oven and heat on high for two minutes.

After two minutes of heating, open the microwave. CAUTION:
THE JUG AND WATER IN THE JUG WILL BE HOT. Quickly but
carefully place the cap on the jug. Make sure the cap is on tightly. Use
a pot holder to remove the jug from the microwave oven. Set the
capped jug on a counter.

Observations

Watch the jug for several minutes. What happens to the sides of
the jug? Does it look like something is pushing in on the sides of the
jug?

Discussion

In a microwave oven, the energy of microwave radiation causes
water molecules to rotate faster. Food containing water cooks be-

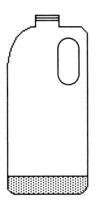 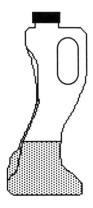

BEFORE HEATING   **AFTER HEATING**

cause the faster rotating water molecules give off heat.

When the water is heated in the microwave oven, some of the water is changed to a gas. Some water molecules gain enough energy to leave the liquid where molecules are close together and become a gas where molecules are farther apart. The water molecules that are changed to a gas fill the plastic jug and push out air molecules.

When the jug is capped, the gas inside is trapped. As the jug cools to room temperature, most of the gas molecules of water change back to a liquid. Since the molecules of water take up less space as a liquid than as a gas, the sides of the jug collapse.

Gaseous water molecules are so far apart that most of the space inside the jug is empty. The jug does not collapse because the gaseous water molecules inside the jug are in constant motion. When the gaseous water molecules cool and change back to a liquid, the remaining gas molecules inside the jug cannot push outward as much as the air molecules in the room are pushing in on the jug. The jug is squeezed together because the air in the room has a greater pressure than the gas inside of the jug.

Other things to try

As the jug cools do you see drops of water form on the inside of the jug? Open the cap of the collapsed jug. Do you hear the sound of air rushing back inside the jug?

Do the walls of the jug spread out to their original position? Once the plastic has been crushed it probably will not go back to its original shape.

Repeat this experiment with another plastic jug using only a teaspoon of water. Does this jug collapse as much as the one containing one-half cup of water?

11 CAN PRESSURE CAUSE ICE TO CHANGE TO LIQUID?

Materials

Water	Two pot holders
An ice tray	A plastic bowl
Refrigerator freezer	

Procedure

Fill an ice tray with water. Place the ice tray in the refrigerator freezer and leave the ice tray overnight. (Ice from automatic ice makers does not work well for this experiment because often the sides of the ice are not flat.)

Remove the ice from the tray and place the ice into the bowl. Place the bowl of ice and the two pot holders in the refrigerator freezer. Wait about ten minutes for the pot holders to get cold.

Remove the pot holders from the freezer. Use the pot holders to remove two ice cubes from the bowl in the freezer. Do not touch the ice with your hands so the ice will not start to melt.

Quickly put one pot holder on the floor. Place one ice cube on the pot holder. Then place the second ice cube on top of the first ice cube. Make sure the flat surfaces of the ice cubes are touching each other.

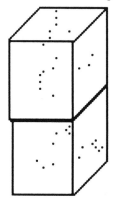

ICE CUBES

Take care not to rub the surfaces of the ice cubes together. Friction from rubbing the ice cubes together can cause the ice on the surface of the ice cubes to melt. Cover the stacked ice cubes with the second pot holder and push straight down on the top pot holder as hard as you can. After about ten seconds stop pushing and remove the top pot holder.

Observations

Are the two cubes stuck together after you press them together? If you pick up one ice cube, does the other ice cube stick to it? If the ice cubes do not stick together, try another pair of ice cubes. You may need to push harder or get an adult to help you push down on the ice cubes. You may have to try this experiment several times.

Discussion

The water molecules in solid ice are slightly farther apart than the water molecules in liquid water. When a large enough pressure is applied to push the water molecules closer together, it causes the ice to melt. When ice melts, it changes from a solid to a liquid.

When the pressure is released, the thin layer of liquid water between the two ice cubes should refreeze back to a solid and the two ice cubes should be frozen together.

Other things to try

Do the two ice cubes remain stuck together? Although the cubes can be broken apart, they tend to melt as one piece.

Try pressing down gently on two ice cubes and then releasing. Do they stick together?

Can you explain why melting ice with pressure is important in ice skating? Try sliding the edge of a dime across a piece of ice. Does it slide easier if you push down on the ice with the dime?

When skating, the weight of a person's body is supported by two thin metal blades. The pressure applied to these metal blades by the weight of a person's body causes the ice underneath them to melt. A skater glides along on a thin layer of liquid. The thin layer of liquid water reduces the friction between the skate blade and the ice. After the skater passes by, the liquid water freezes back to a solid ice.

DOES THE ICE ON A FROSTED GLASS MELT FROM THE TOP TO THE BOTTOM OR FROM THE BOTTOM TO THE TOP? **12**

Materials

Two tall, clear glasses

A paper towel

A refrigerator freezer

Procedure

Place two tall, clear glasses in the freezer. Leave the glasses in the freezer for several hours. Open the freezer and remove one of the glasses with a paper towel. Place the glass upside down on the countertop. Remove the other glass using the paper towel. Place this glass rightside up on the countertop. Close the freezer door. Observe the glasses for about ten minutes.

If the glasses do not become frosted when you remove them from the freezer, repeat the experiment using glasses that have been rinsed in water.

FROSTED GLASSES

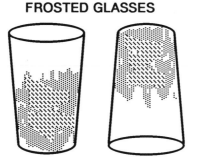

Observations

Are the glasses frosted after you leave them in the freezer for several hours? Do the glasses become more frosted when you remove them from the freezer? Does the frost on the glass placed upside down melt from the top to the bottom or from the bottom to the top? Does the frost on the glass placed rightside up melt from the top to the bottom or from the bottom to the top?

Discussion

Frost is made of tiny ice crystals. The tiny ice crystals form when water molecules in the air condense and freeze on a cold surface. Water molecules in the air change from a gas to a liquid when they condense. When water freezes, water molecules change from a liquid to a solid.

The cold glasses should have very little frost on them when they are in the freezer because there should be fewer water molecules in the air in a freezer. When the glasses are removed from the freezer, water molecules in the room air condense and freeze on the cold glasses. The glasses should become more frosted when you remove them from the freezer.

When the frost melts, the water molecules in the tiny ice crystals change from a solid to a liquid. The frost on the glasses melts because the glasses become warmer. The glasses become warmer because the room is warmer than the freezer.

Most glasses are made so that the glass becomes thicker as you move from the top of the glass to the bottom of the glass. The thinner part of the glasses becomes warmer faster than the thicker part of the glasses. Since the thinner part of the glasses becomes warmer faster, the frost should start to melt at the thinner part of the glasses. The frost on the glass placed rightside up should melt from the top to the bottom, and the frost on the glass placed upside down should melt from the bottom to the top.

Other things to try

Repeat this experiment with different glasses. Try using glasses with different shapes. Do you get similar results?

DOES SHORTENING BECOME CLEAR WHEN IT MELTS?   **13**

Materials
Shortening (such as Crisco)   A tablespoon
A stove   An aluminum pie pan
A small saucepan

Procedure
ASK AN ADULT TO HELP YOU WITH THIS EXPERIMENT. DO NOT USE THE STOVE BY YOURSELF.

Place one tablespoon of shortening in a small saucepan. Observe the appearance of the shortening. Set the stove burner on low heat. Heat the saucepan on the stove burner until the shortening completely melts. Turn off the stove. Remove the saucepan from the heat and carefully pour the melted shortening into an aluminum pie pan. Observe the appearance of the melted shortening. Allow the shortening to cool. Observe the appearance of the cooled shortening.

SOLID SHORTENING

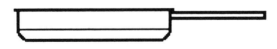

MELTED SHORTENING

Observations
Is the shortening clear or cloudy before you melt it on the stove? Is the shortening clear or cloudy after you completely melt it? Does

the melted shortening become cloudy or clear after it cools?

Discussion

Shortening is a fat. Fats are large molecules made of carbon, hydrogen, and oxygen atoms. Fats are a solid at room temperature because the fat molecules stick to each other and pack closely together.

When light hits a collection of solid fat molecules, the light is scattered. The closely packed fat molecules in a solid scatter the light so that the light no longer moves in a straight path. This is why the shortening is not clear.

Fat molecules move faster and farther apart when fat melts. The fat becomes a liquid when it melts. Much of the light can pass through the liquid fat molecules because the molecules are farther apart. This is why the shortening looks clear when it melts. When the shortening cools and becomes a solid again, the closely packed fat molecules scatter the light. The solid shortening should no longer be clear.

Other things to try

Heat a tablespoon of butter in a small saucepan over low heat until most of the butter melts. Not all of the butter will melt. Is most of the melted butter clear or cloudy? Let the melted butter cool. Does the butter become cloudy or clear after it cools?

Is bacon grease clear when it is a liquid and cloudy when it is a solid? Do you understand why?

ARE OIL AND GREASE MOLECULES SLIPPERY?

Materials

A piece of wax paper   A pencil with an eraser

A paper towel   Petroleum jelly (such as Vaseline)

Household machine oil (such as 3-IN-ONE)

Procedure

Place a piece of wax paper on a flat table. Hold the pencil so that the eraser is touching the wax paper. Practice pushing the pencil across the wax paper. Change the position of the pencil in your hand until you find the best position of the pencil for the pencil eraser to skip rapidly across the wax paper.

Place several drops of household machine oil on the wax paper. Pass through the drops of oil as you push the pencil eraser across the wax paper. What happens when the eraser moves through the oil?

Wipe the oil off the pencil eraser with a paper towel. Place some petroleum jelly on the wax paper. Pass through the petroleum jelly as you push the pencil across the wax paper. What happens when the eraser moves through the petroleum jelly?

Observations

Does the eraser move more easily over the wax paper after it passes through the oil? Does the eraser move more easily over the wax paper after it passes through the petroleum jelly?

Discussion

When two objects rub against each other friction is created. Friction is a resistance to movement. Friction is created between two objects because the surfaces of the two objects tend to stick together. Friction is created when you move the pencil eraser across the wax

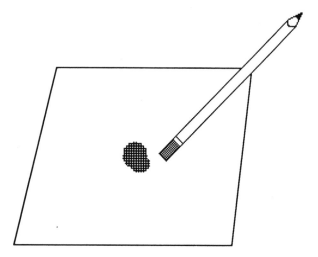

PENCIL ERASER PUSHED ACROSS
WAX PAPER WITH OIL ON IT

paper. The pencil eraser wants to stick to the wax paper. This is why the pencil eraser skips across the wax paper.

Oil and grease can reduce friction between two objects that rub together. Oil and grease make objects move more easily over each other. Oil and grease are lubricants. Lubricants are substances that are slippery.

When oil or grease is placed between two objects, there is a thin layer of oil or grease molecules between the two objects. The oil or grease molecules keep the two objects from touching each other. The two objects can no longer stick to each other. Oil or grease molecules move over each other easily. This is why oil and grease molecules are slippery.

When the pencil eraser moves through the oil on the wax paper, a thin layer of oil molecules separates the pencil eraser from the wax paper. The pencil eraser should move more easily over the wax paper when the layer of oil molecules is between the pencil eraser and the wax paper.

Do you understand now why you need to add oil or grease to the moving parts of a bicycle or car?

Other things to try

Rub your finger across a piece of clean wax paper. Place some petroleum jelly on the wax paper. Rub your finger in the petroleum jelly and move across the wax paper. Does your finger move more easily across the wax paper when it has petroleum jelly on it?

15 DO DETERGENT MOLECULES HELP CLEAN CLOTHES?

Materials

Tide or other clothes detergent	Water
Black shoe polish	A measuring cup
A piece of scrap white cloth	A teaspoon
Two zip-lock bags	Scissors
Clock	

Procedure

Get an adult to help you cut a piece of scrap white cloth (part of an old T-shirt, for example) into two small pieces. Each piece should be about two inches square or about the size of the palm of your hand.

Touch the middle of each piece of cloth to the shoe polish to get a black spot on the cloth. Be careful not to get any shoe polish on you. Fold the cloth over the spot of polish and rub the cloth to spread the spot to about the size of a penny.

Unfold each piece of cloth and place it in a zip-lock bag. Add one teaspoon of Tide or other clothes detergent to one bag. Now add one-half cup of water to both bags. Close each bag and pull your fingers across the top of the bag so the bag is locked shut. Shake the two bags for about one minute and then set them in a sink. Wait 30 minutes. Open each bag and remove the pieces of cloth.

Observations

Does the water in the bag with detergent turn dark? Does the water in the bag with no detergent turn dark?

SPOT ON CLOTH AFTER CLEANING

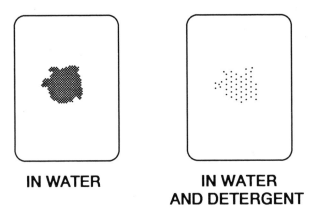

IN WATER   **IN WATER
                                AND DETERGENT**

Which cloth is cleaner? Did the detergent help clean the cloth?

Discussion

A synthetic detergent molecule has polar and nonpolar ends. The polar end of a detergent molecule is attracted to water because water is polar. The nonpolar end of a detergent molecule is attracted to nonpolar substances such as grease, wax, and oil.

The presence of detergent molecules in water allows shoe polish wax to mix with water. Detergents help to remove grease, oil, and wax from clothes by making these nonpolar substances mix with water. Without detergent in the water, the shoe polish wax tends to stick on the cloth. Nonpolar substances are not removed from cloth by water alone.

Other things to try

Repeat this experiment using grape jelly instead of shoe polish.

Is the grape jelly stain removed by water and detergent? Is the grape jelly stain removed by just water?

Grape jelly includes polar molecules that will mix with water. Detergent may not be necessary to clean stains that readily mix with water.

Repeat this experiment with shoe polish. In one bag use detergent in hot water. In one bag use detergent in cold water. Does detergent in hot water clean better than detergent in cold water?

CAN SUGAR MOLECULES MAKE SOAP BUBBLES LAST LONGER? 16

Materials

Sugar	A teaspoon
A watch or clock	A bowl
Soap bubble liquid and ring	Pencil and paper

You can buy bottles of soap bubble mix in toy stores and in many grocery stores. These bottles usually include a ring to blow bubbles. If you choose, you can make soap bubble solution from Joy dishwashing liquid and water. Mix one teaspoon of dishwashing liquid and nine teaspoons of water together. You can make a ring from a paper clip or a piece of wire. Bend the wire or paper clip to make a small loop on one end.

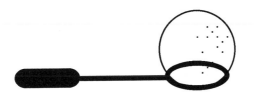

Procedure

Blow a bubble with the soap mixture and catch it on the ring. Look at the time on a watch or clock. Hold the ring and watch the bubble. When the bubble breaks, check the time and write down how long the bubble lasts before breaking. Repeat this several times.

Add two level teaspoons of sugar to the bowl. Add five teaspoons of soap bubble liquid to the bowl. Stir the mixture until all the sugar dissolves (goes into the liquid). If all the sugar will not dissolve, add a little more soap bubble liquid.

Blow a bubble with the sugar-soap mixture and catch it on the ring. Look at the time on a watch or clock. Hold the ring and watch the bubble. When the bubble breaks, check the time and write down the lifetime of the bubble. Repeat this several times.

Observations

How long do the regular soap bubbles usually last before they break? How long do the soap bubbles containing sugar usually last before they break? Which type of bubble lasts longer?

Discussion

Soap bubbles are made of soap molecules and water molecules. A soap molecule has a polar and nonpolar end. Water is a polar molecule. The polar ends of soap molecules are attracted to the polar ends of water molecules. The nonpolar ends of the soap molecules are attracted to each other. The nonpolar ends of the soap molecules stick out of the water and help to hold the bubble together. Water molecules and soap or other similar molecules are necessary to form the thin surface of a bubble.

As the water in the bubble evaporates or goes from a liquid to a gas, the wall of the bubble gets thinner and finally the bubble breaks.

Table sugar is made of sucrose molecules. Each sucrose molecule contains 12 carbon, 22 hydrogen, and 11 oxygen atoms. Each water molecule is made of two hydrogen atoms bonded to one oxygen atom. Sucrose molecules are attracted to water molecules because of the arrangement of the atoms in the sucrose molecule. The attraction between the sucrose molecules and the water molecules helps to keep the water molecules from leaving the soap bubble and going into the air. By keeping the water molecules in the soap bubble, the lifetime of the soap bubble is increased.

Other things to try

Repeat this experiment with different amounts of sugar and soap solution. Try more or less sugar and see if you can find the best amounts to make the bubbles last a long time.

Fructose is another type of sugar that is available. It is a smaller sugar molecule than sucrose. Mix soap bubble liquid with fructose and compare the lifetime of bubbles made with fructose to those made with sucrose.

Repeat this experiment, but watch the bubbles closely as they break. Do the regular soap bubbles break apart in one quick burst? Do the sugar soap bubbles break apart gradually and seem to collapse while the surface stays together? Can you explain any differences you observe?

17 DO SOAP MOLECULES SPREAD OUT MORE SLOWLY ON THE SURFACE OF WATER OR OIL?

Materials

Two plates	Dishwashing liquid
Water	Pepper
Cooking oil	

Procedure

Set each plate on a table. Pour water into one plate until it is full of water. Pour cooking oil into the second plate until it is full of oil. Sprinkle pepper all over the surface of the water and the oil.

Allow one drop of dishwashing liquid to fall to the center of the plate of oil. Allow one drop of oil to fall to the center of the plate of water. Watch the pepper on each plate.

DROP OF SOAP SPREADING

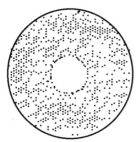

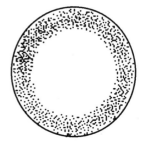

PEPPER ON OIL   PEPPER ON WATER

Observations

What happens to the pepper? Does the pepper spread out toward the outside of each plate? In which plate does the pepper spread out more slowly?

Discussion

A water molecule is made of two hydrogen atoms and one oxygen atom. This combination of atoms makes water molecules polar. There are two ends to a water molecule. One end has a slight negative charge and the other end has a slight positive charge.

Oil molecules are made of mostly carbon and hydrogen atoms. This combination of atoms makes oil nonpolar. Nonpolar means there are no charges on the molecules.

Soap molecules are made of a short polar end and a long nonpolar end. The polar end of the soap molecule is attracted to water because water molecules are polar. The nonpolar end of the soap molecule is attracted to oil because oil molecules are nonpolar. When a drop of soap is added to water, it spreads out across the surface of the water. The polar end of the soap molecule goes into the water. The nonpolar end of the soap molecule sticks out of the water.

When a drop of soap is added to oil, it spreads out across the surface of the oil. The long nonpolar end of the soap molecule goes into the oil. The polar end of the soap molecule sticks out of the oil.

Soap can spread out on the surface of either water or oil. The soap can spread until it forms a layer only one molecule thick on the surface of oil or water. As the soap molecules spread out, the pepper is pushed out across the surface toward the edge of the plate.

Soap spreads more slowly across the surface of the oil than the water. It should only take about a second for the pepper to be pushed to the edge of the plate of water. It may take about a minute for the pepper to be pushed to the edge of the plate of oil. The reason the soap spreads more rapidly across the water is because there is a stronger attraction between soap and oil molecules than between soap and water molecules.

Other things to try

Repeat this experiment using liquid hand soap. Compare the speed of spreading on oil and water.

Try dipping a bar of soap in the middle of a plate of water covered with pepper. Does the soap gradually spread out across the water? Try dipping a bar of soap in the middle of a plate of oil covered with pepper. Does the soap spread out across the oil as fast or as much as with the water?

DO SMALL PARTICLES REACT FASTER THAN LARGE PARTICLES IN A CHEMICAL REACTION?

Materials

Two clear glasses	Two tablespoons
Water	Tape
Two Alka-Seltzer tablets	A felt pen

Procedure

Place a piece of tape on each glass. Write "crushed" on one piece of tape and "whole" on the other piece of tape. Fill each glass with the same amount of water. Set each glass on a table.

Carefully crush one of the Alka-Seltzer tablets between two tablespoons until it is a fine powder. At the same time, add the crushed Alka-Seltzer tablet to the glass of water labeled "crushed" and add the whole Alka-Seltzer tablet to the glass of water labeled "whole." Watch both glasses.

DO NOT DRINK THE ALKA-SELTZER WATER. Alka-Seltzer tablets are medicine and should not be taken by a child or young person unless advised by a doctor.

ALKA-SELTZER TABLETS IN WATER

CRUSHED   WHOLE

Observations

Do you see bubbles in each glass? Which glass produces more bubbles — the one with the whole tablet or the one with the crushed tablet? Which glass produces bubbles for the shorter time? Which glass produces bubbles for the longer time?

Discussion

A chemical reaction occurs when an Alka-Seltzer tablet is added to water. In a chemical reaction atoms undergo a rearrangement to make new chemical substances. One of the new chemical substances made when an Alka-Seltzer tablet and water undergo a chemical reaction is carbon dioxide gas. The bubbles you see when an Alka-Seltzer tablet reacts with water are carbon dioxide gas.

The chemical substances in an Alka-Seltzer tablet must come in contact with water molecules for a chemical reaction to occur between the Alka-Seltzer tablet and water. When the crushed Alka-Seltzer tablet is added to water, more of the chemical substances in the tablet can come into contact with water molecules because the tablet is in smaller pieces. The chemical reaction should be faster when the crushed Alka-Seltzer tablet is added to water. You should see gas bubbles appear more quickly when the crushed tablet is added to water, and the crushed tablet should disappear more quickly.

Has anyone ever told you to chew your food well before you swallow it? Have you ever wondered why you were told to do this? Food in your stomach is broken down into small molecules which your body can use for energy and building other molecules. The food is broken down by chemical substances in your stomach. The chemical substances in your stomach break down food in a chemical reaction. This chemical reaction is called digestion. Small food particles will break down into smaller molecules faster than large food particles. Your food will be digested faster if you chew your food into smaller particles.

Other things to try

Break an Alka-Seltzer tablet into several pieces. Does the Alka-Seltzer tablet broken in pieces react faster than a whole tablet?

Add a crushed Alka-Seltzer tablet to hot water from the sink faucet. How long does it take for all the crushed tablet to react with the hot water?

19 IS LESS LIGHT EMITTED FROM A"LIGHTSTICK" AT COLDER TEMPERATURES?

Materials

Two chemical lightsticks	Ice
A large bowl	Tape
A dark room or closet	A felt pen
Water	A paper towel

Chemical lightsticks may be purchased in many large sporting goods stores and hardware stores. They are also called Glow Stick and Cyalume Lightsticks.

Procedure

CAREFULLY READ THE LABEL ON THE PROTECTIVE WRAP-PER OF THE CHEMICAL LIGHTSTICK. Remove the chemical lightsticks from their protective wrappers. Do not bend the tubes until instructed to do so below. Place a piece of tape on each lightstick. Write "cold" on one piece of tape and "room temperature" on the other.

Place the chemical lightstick labeled "cold" in a large bowl. Cover the lightstick with ice. Add water until the lightstick is completely covered with water. Leave the lightstick in the ice water for one hour.

Remove the lightstick labeled "cold" from the ice water and dry it with a paper towel. Take both lightsticks into a dark room or closet. Bend both lightsticks until you feel a snap in each. Shake both lightsticks and make your observations.

Allow the lightstick labeled "cold" to warm to room temperature. This may take thirty minutes or more. Is the same amount of light emitted from both lightsticks now?

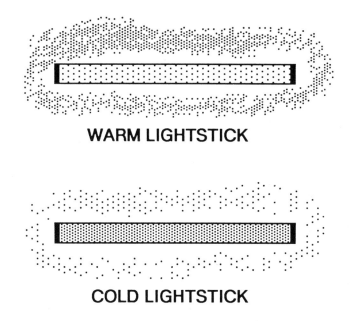

WARM LIGHTSTICK

COLD LIGHTSTICK

Place the lightstick labeled "cold" back into the bowl of ice water. Is less light emitted from this lightstick as it becomes cold again?

Observations

What color is the light that is emitted from your lightsticks? Is less light emitted from the lightstick labeled "cold" or "room temperature?" Is the same amount of light emitted from both lightsticks when the lightstick labeled "cold" is warmed to room temperature? Is less light emitted from the lightstick labeled "cold" when it becomes cold again?

Discussion

Chemical substances, like molecules, are changed into other chemical substances in a <u>chemical reaction</u>. There are also energy changes in a chemical reaction. Most chemical reactions occur with a change in <u>heat energy</u>. For example, some chemical reactions give off heat and are hot. Some chemical reactions absorb heat energy and are cold. There are a few chemical reactions in which light energy is produced. These chemical reactions are called chemiluminescent reactions. Fireflies make light by a chemiluminescent reaction. In living organisms that make light, the chemiluminescent reaction is called bioluminescence.

In this reaction you are using the amount of light emitted by the lightsticks to determine how fast a chemical reaction occurs. The faster the reaction occurs in the lightstick, the more light you should see. The slower the reaction occurs in the lightstick, the less light you should see.

For a chemical reaction to occur between different molecules, the different molecules must hit each other. They must hit hard enough to cause the atoms in the different molecules to undergo a rearrangement. This rearrangement gives new molecules or chemical substances.

Hot molecules move faster and have more energy than cold molecules. Atoms in hot molecules can rearrange faster than atoms in cold molecules. Hot molecules react faster than cold molecules. This is why more light is emitted from the lightstick labeled "room temperature" than from the lightstick labeled "cold." The different molecules in the lightstick labeled "room temperature" are hotter and have more energy than the different molecules in the lightstick labeled "cold." The chemical reaction is faster in the lightstick labeled "room temperature."

A chemical reaction occurs when foods are cooked. We use heat from a stove to cause the chemical reaction in cooking to occur faster.

Food also spoils by chemical reactions. We store food in the refrigerator and freezer to slow down or stop the chemical reaction that causes food to spoil.

Other things to try

Do you think a lightstick kept cold will emit light longer than a lightstick kept at room temperature? How can you find out?

20 CAN MOLECULES IN SUNSCREENS BLOCK LIGHT FROM THE SUN THAT CAUSES COLORS TO FADE?

Materials

Blue construction paper   Tape

Plastic food wrap

Solid objects such as coins, paper clips, and pencils

Sunscreen with an SPF rating of 30 or greater (SPF stands

 for sun protection factor)

Procedure

Tape a piece of plastic food wrap on the blue construction paper. The plastic food wrap should cover about half of the construction paper. Place a drop of sunscreen with an SPF rating of 30 or greater on the plastic wrap. With a circular motion, use your finger to spread the sunscreen on the plastic wrap in a circle. The circle of thin sunscreen should be about the size of your fist.

Place the piece of construction paper outside on a bright sunny day. Set several solid objects on the plastic film and on the blue construction paper that is not covered by the plastic film. Do not put any objects on top of the sunscreen.

Leave the construction paper in the bright sun for several hours. Remove one of the solid objects from the blue construction paper that is not covered with plastic film. If the paper has not faded, place the solid object back on the construction paper and leave the construction paper in the bright sun for several more hours. When the blue construction paper has faded, remove all the solid objects and the plastic film. Make your observations.

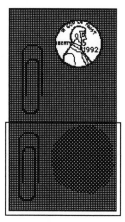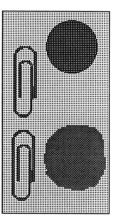

COLORED PAPER
AND PLASTIC WRAP
WITH SUNSCREEN
BEFORE EXPOSURE
TO SUNLIGHT

COLORED PAPER
AFTER EXPOSURE
TO SUNLIGHT

Observations

Is the sunscreen a creamy white color when you spread it on the plastic film? Does the sunscreen become clear after about thirty minutes?

How long does it take for the construction paper to fade? Does the part of the construction paper under the solid objects fade? Does the part of the construction paper under the plastic film coated with sunscreen fade? Is the construction paper under the plastic film coated with sunscreen as faded as the construction under the plastic film not coated with sunscreen? Is the construction paper under the plastic film coated with sunscreen as faded as the construction paper not covered with the plastic film?

Discussion

The blue color in the construction paper placed in the sun fades because of a chemical reaction. Oxygen molecules in the air react with blue dye molecules in the paper. The chemical reaction between oxygen molecules and the blue dye molecules changes the blue dye molecules. The blue dye molecules are changed into molecules that are colorless or that have very little color. When oxygen molecules change other molecules in a chemical reaction the reaction is called an oxidation reaction.

Sunlight is needed for the chemical reaction to occur between the oxygen molecules and the blue dye molecules. The sunlight makes the oxygen molecules more reactive. The blue construction paper under the solid objects does not fade because the solid objects block the sunlight.

The blue construction paper under the plastic film should fade. The sunlight can pass through the plastic film and make the oxygen molecules under it more reactive. The blue construction paper under the plastic film coated with sunscreen should not be as faded as the construction paper under the plastic film. Molecules in the sunscreen block or absorb some of the sunlight that makes oxygen molecules more reactive. Not all of the sunlight that makes oxygen molecules more reactive is blocked by the sunscreen. This is why the blue construction paper under the plastic film coated with sunscreen does fade a little.

Sunscreens can protect people from getting sunburn. Molecules in the sunscreens absorb some of the light from the sun that causes sunburn.

Other things to try

Repeat this experiment with other colors of construction paper. Do you get similar results?

Repeat this experiment with sunscreens with a SPF rating lower than 10. Do you get similar results?

When you are spreading the sunscreen on the plastic wrap, write your name with the sunscreen. Can you see your name on the construction paper after the paper has faded?

IS AIR NECESSARY
FOR PAINT TO BECOME HARD?

Materials

Oil-based paint	A piece of white paper
Old newspapers	A pen or pencil
Two small pieces of wood	Tape

A disposable aluminum pie pan or a piece of aluminum foil

A plastic bag which can be tightly sealed (such as a zip-lock bag)

Procedure

ASK AN ADULT TO HELP YOU WITH THIS EXPERIMENT. DO THIS EXPERIMENT OUTSIDE OR IN A GARAGE. PAINT IS MESSY AND HARD TO CLEAN UP.

Place some old newspapers on a work table or cardboard box. Write "WET PAINT" on a piece of white paper. Tape this piece of paper on the newspapers where people can see it. Open the can of oil-based paint. Stir the paint with one of the small pieces of wood for a few seconds. Remove the small piece of wood from the paint and hold it over the paint can until the excess paint stops dripping off. Slide the aluminum pie pan under the wood. Place the pie pan with the piece of wood in it on the newspapers.

Take the second piece of wood and stir the paint for a few seconds. Make sure to use a piece of wood that will fit in the plastic bag. Remove the small piece of wood from the paint and hold it over the paint can until the excess paint stops dripping off. Place the wood in the plastic bag. Squeeze most of the air out of the bag and tightly seal the bag. The sides of the plastic bag should touch the wood and paint. Place the bag on the newspapers. Let the experiment sit for twenty-four hours. If the painted piece of wood in

PAINTED WOOD IN SEALED PLASTIC BAG

PAINTED WOOD IN ALUMINUM PIE PAN

the pie pan is still wet, let the experiment sit for another twenty-four hours.

Observations

When the painted piece of wood in the pie pan is dry, is the painted piece of wood sealed in the plastic bag dry, or is it still wet? Does the painted piece of wood sealed in the plastic bag become dry after several days?

Discussion

Oil-based paint is made mostly of linseed oil, pigment, and paint thinner. The pigment is what gives the paint color. The paint thinner keeps the paint from getting too thick so that the paint spreads thinly and evenly on a surface. The paint thinner evaporates after the paint is put on a surface. The linseed oil is what makes the paint hard when it dries.

Linseed oil molecules are large molecules made of carbon, hydrogen, and oxygen molecules. Oxygen molecules in the air can react with linseed oil molecules. Linseed oil molecules join together to make a polymer when they react with oxygen molecules. Polymers are large molecules made by joining smaller molecules together in chains. The process of joining smaller molecules into a polymer is called polymerization. The polymer made by joining linseed oil molecules together is called a film. This film is very hard and gives the painted surface a protective coating. Pigment molecules are trapped in the film and can only be removed by removing the film.

In this experiment, the paint on the piece of wood in the aluminum pie pan should become hard before the paint on the piece of wood in the plastic bag. The paint on the piece of wood in the aluminum pie pan is surrounded by more oxygen molecules than the paint on the piece of wood in the plastic bag. This causes the linseed oil molecules in the paint in the aluminum pie pan to join together faster than the linseed oil molecules in the paint in the plastic bag. The paint on the piece of wood in the the plastic bag should become hard after several days because there are some oxygen molecules in the bag when you seal the bag.

Other things to try

Repeat this experiment with a latex paint. Do you get similar results? Latex paints do not react with oxygen molecules to form a polymer. Latex paints already have polymer molecules in them when they are made. When you paint a surface with latex paint you are spreading the latex paint polymer over the surface. When the paint thinner—which is usually water for latex paints—evaporates, the latex polymer and pigment remain on the painted surface.

22 CAN GROUND GINGER CAUSE YEAST TO PRODUCE CARBON DIOXIDE GAS FROM SUGARS MORE RAPIDLY?

Materials

Yeast	A shallow pan
Sugar	Two large balloons
Ground ginger	Warm water
Measuring spoons	Tape
A two-cup measuring cup	A felt pen
A one-half cup measuring cup	Two empty soft drink bottles

Procedure

Fill the two-cup measuring cup with one cup of warm water from the sink faucet. Make sure the water is warm but not hot. Add one teaspoon of sugar. Stir until the sugar dissolves. Add one tablespoon or one packet of yeast to the warm sugar water. Stir for about one minute to dissolve the yeast. Make sure all the yeast is dissolved before you begin the experiment.

Place a piece of tape on each bottle. Write "ginger" on one piece of tape and "no ginger" on the other.

Fill a shallow pan with warm water from the sink faucet. Use a shallow pan that will hold the two drink bottles.

Use the one-half cup measuring cup to pour one-half cup of the yeast solution into each bottle. Add one-fourth teaspoon of ground ginger to the bottle labeled "ginger." Gently shake each bottle to mix the solutions. Quickly slip a large, deflated balloon over the top of each bottle. Make sure the large balloons are the same size. Also, make sure there is very little air in the balloons when you slip them on the bottles. Place the bottles in the pan of warm water. Observe which balloon stands up on the bottle first.

After each balloon stands up on the bottle, remove the balloons. Slip the deflated balloons back on the bottles. Again, observe which balloon stands up on the bottle first.

WATER, SUGAR,
AND YEAST

WATER, SUGAR,
GINGER, AND YEAST

Observations

What color is the yeast mixture? Can you smell the yeast? Can you see bubbles forming in the yeast mixture in the bottles? Do the balloons become inflated? Which balloon stands up first—the one labeled "ginger" or "no ginger?"

Discussion

Yeast is a simple living system containing one cell that can break down sugar molecules into smaller molecules. These smaller molecules are carbon dioxide gas and ethyl alcohol. Yeast breaks down sugar molecules by a chemical reaction. This chemical reaction is called fermentation.

In this experiment you are using yeast to break down table sugar.

Sucrose is the chemical name for table sugar. The carbon dioxide gas that is made in the fermentation reaction is trapped in the balloons.

Ground ginger can cause the yeast to break down sugar molecules faster. Carbon dioxide molecules are made faster in the bottle labeled "ginger" than in the bottle labeled "no ginger." The balloon on the bottle labeled "ginger" should stand up first. The fermentation reaction is faster when ground ginger is added to the yeast mixture.

It is not known how ginger causes yeast to break down sugar molecules faster. Scientists have theories as to how ginger causes the fermentation reaction to be faster. A theory is an educated guess or model of how something works. One theory on how ginger causes the fermentation reaction to be faster is that certain chemicals in ginger make the yeast break down sugar molecules faster. Another theory says that the ground ginger keeps the yeast cells from clumping together. Fermentation is slower when yeast cells clump together.

Scientists test theories by doing experiments. To test the theories on how ginger causes yeast to break down sugar molecules faster, more experiments need to be performed. Maybe someday new experiments will give us a better understanding of how ginger causes yeast to break down sugar molecules faster.

Other things to try

Repeat this experiment with two teaspoons of sugar. Do you get similar results?

Ground ginger is a type of spice. Repeat this experiment with other ground spices such as thyme, pepper, and oregano. Do you get similar results?

CAN LARGE MOLECULES SCATTER LIGHT? 23

Materials

One packet of unflavored gelatin	Measuring spoons
Table sugar	Spoons for stirring
Water	A flashlight
A two-cup measuring cup	Tape
A one-cup measuring cup	A felt pen
Three tall, clean, clear glasses	

Procedure

Place a piece of tape on each glass. Label the glasses "gelatin," "sugar," and "water." Add one cup of water from the sink faucet to the glass labeled "water." Add one cup of water from the sink faucet to the glass labeled "sugar." Add one teaspoon of sugar to the water in the glass labeled "sugar." Stir with a spoon to dissolve the sugar.

Add one-half cup of cold water to the two-cup measuring cup. Open the packet of unflavored gelatin and add one teaspoon of the gelatin to the cold water in the two-cup measuring cup. Stir the gelatin and water with a spoon for thirty seconds. All of the gelatin will not dissolve in the cold water. Carefully fill the two-cup measuring cup containing the gelatin and water with hot water from the sink faucet. Stir the gelatin solution with a spoon for thirty seconds. Let the hot gelatin solution sit for thirty minutes to cool. Carefully pour one cup of the gelatin solution into the glass labeled "gelatin."

Take the flashlight and the three labeled glasses into a dark room. Turn on the flashlight and shine the light through the glass labeled "gelatin." You may need to put the flashlight against the glass. What do you see? Shine the light through the glasses labeled "water" and "sugar." What do you see?

Let the glass labeled "gelatin" sit for several days. Shine the light from a flashlight through the gelatin solution while in a dark room. Can you still see the beam of light from the flashlight pass through the gelatin solution?

SUGAR SOLUTION **GELATIN SOLUTION**

FLASHLIGHT

Observations

Is the gelatin solution clear or cloudy? Is the sugar solution clear or cloudy? Is the water clear or cloudy? Can you see the light beam from the flashlight pass through the solution labeled "gelatin?" Can you see the light beam from the flashlight pass through the solution labeled "water" and "sugar?" Can you see the light beam from the flashlight pass through the gelatin solution after the gelatin solution sits for several days?

Discussion

Some molecules are small and some molecules are quite large. In this experiment you are using light to compare the sizes of different molecules that dissolve in water. You are comparing the sizes of water and table sugar molecules with protein molecules from gelatin.

<u>Protein</u> molecules are polymers. <u>Polymers</u> are large molecules

made by joining smaller molecules together in long chains. The smaller molecules joined together to make proteins are called amino acids. Gelatin is a type of protein.

Sucrose is the chemical name for table sugar. Sucrose molecules contain twelve carbon atoms, twenty-two hydrogen atoms, and eleven oxygen atoms. A water molecule is made of two hydrogen atoms and one oxygen atom. The protein molecules in gelatin are much larger than water molecules and sucrose molecules. The protein molecules in gelatin contain thousands of atoms of mostly carbon, hydrogen, oxygen, and nitrogen.

The gelatin solution should appear clear. Although we can not see the individual protein molecules in the gelatin solution because they are too small, they are large enough to scatter light. When light is scattered by particles, the light beam can be seen. You should be able to see the light beam from the flashlight when you shine the light through the gelatin solution. The protein molecules in the gelatin solution scatter the light. Water molecules and sucrose molecules are too small to scatter light. You should not be able to see the light beam from the flashlight when you shine the light through the water or the sugar solution.

You should still be able to see the light beam pass through the gelatin solution after the gelatin solution sits for several days. The protein molecules in gelatin are not large enough to be pulled to the bottom of the glass by gravity. The protein molecules stay suspended in the water. A gelatin solution is an example of a colloid. A colloid is made when tiny particles that scatter light stay suspended in a gas or liquid. Some other examples of colloids include milk, paint, butter, cheese, whipped cream, smoke, and fog.

Other things to try

Add one drop of milk to one cup of water in a tall, clear glass. While in a dark room, shine the light from a flashlight through the dilute milk solution. Can you see the light beam from the flashlight pass through the dilute milk solution? You should see it because some of the molecules in milk are large and will scatter light.

ARE STARCH MOLECULES LARGER THAN SUGAR MOLECULES? **24**

Materials

A measuring cup   Water

Two clear glasses or jars   Two teaspoons

Cornstarch   Sugar

Procedure

Add one cup of water to each glass. Add one teaspoon of cornstarch to first glass. Stir the cornstarch and water for about thirty seconds. Add one teaspoon of sugar to the second glass. Stir the sugar and water for about thirty seconds.

Hold both glasses up to a window or light and try to look through them.

SUGAR IN WATER   STARCH IN WATER

Observations

Can you see through the sugar and water mixture? Can you see through the cornstarch and water mixture? Is the sugar and water clear and colorless? Is the cornstarch and water a white cloudy color?

Discussion

Table sugar is made of <u>sucrose</u> molecules. Each sucrose molecule has several hydroxyl groups on it. A hydroxyl (OH) is an oxygen and hydrogen atom linked together. Hydroxyl groups are similar to water which has two hydrogens attached to an oxygen. Hydroxyl groups in molecules are attracted to water molecules.

When sucrose is placed in water, water molecules are attracted to the hydroxyl groups on sucrose. The sucrose breaks down into individual molecules surrounded by water molecules. Light passes through a solution of sugar and water, and this is why the sugar and water mixture is clear.

Starch is a very large molecule made of long, branched chains of glucose molecules linked together. A single starch molecule may consist of thousands of glucose molecules joined together. Starch molecules have many hydroxyl groups, but because the starch molecule is so large, it is not soluble in water. It does not break down into individual starch molecules surrounded by water. Rather, it forms clumps of starch molecules which tend to stay together. The starch and water mixture does not let the light pass through it and so it has a white cloudy color.

Other things to try

Fructose is a type of sugar found in many fruits and is sometimes used as a sweetener. Fructose is available in grocery stores. When the small fructose molecules are added to water would you expect the liquid to be clear or cloudy? Repeat this experiment using fructose. Can you see through a fructose and water mixture?

Milk is made of clumps of protein and fat in water. Can you explain why you cannot see through milk?

CAN HEAT BE USED TO BREAK STARCH INTO SMALLER MOLECULES? **25**

Materials

Aluminum foil	Water
An oven	Two teaspoons
Cornstarch	Two clear glasses
A metal cookie sheet	A pot holder
A measuring cup	

Procedure

ASK AN ADULT TO HELP YOU. DO NOT USE THE OVEN BY YOURSELF.

Set the oven on 475° Fahrenheit. Put a piece of aluminum foil on the metal cookie sheet. Spread three teaspoons of cornstarch on the aluminum foil. Put the cookie sheet in the oven and close the oven.

Wait no more than twenty minutes. If most of the cornstarch has been changed to a dark brown solid, then turn the oven off. If the aluminum foil is still covered with mostly cornstarch then heat for five more minutes. After a few minutes check again. If the sheet is left in the oven too long, the solid may char and turn black. Use a pot holder to remove the cookie sheet from the oven and place the cookie sheet on the stove. Do not touch the cookie sheet until it has cooled. Turn the oven off.

Add one cup of water to each glass. Add one-half teaspoon of cornstarch to the first glass. Stir the cornstarch and water for about one minute.

Crush some of the brown solid on the cookie sheet into a powder. Add one-half teaspoon of the brown solid to the second glass. Stir the brown solid and water for about one minute.

STARCH BEFORE HEATING

AFTER HEATING - DEXTRIN

Hold both glasses up to a window or light and try to look through them.

Observations

What color is cornstarch? Did the heat change some of the cornstarch to a dark brown solid?

Is the water in the glass containing cornstarch a white cloudy color? Can you see through the cornstarch and water mixture? Is the other solution brown but clear? Can you see through the brown water mixture?

Discussion

Starch is a large molecule made of long branched chains of glucose molecules linked together. Glucose is a type of sugar molecule. A single starch molecule may consist of thousands of glucose molecules joined together.

When starch is heated it breaks down into smaller molecules called dextrin. Dextrin molecules are small chains of glucose molecules linked together. Dextrin molecules can contain as few as seven or eight glucose molecules joined together.

Because the starch molecule is so large, starch does not break down into individual starch molecules surrounded by water. Instead, starch tends to form clumps of molecules which stay together. Larger clumps of solid gradually settle to the bottom of the liquid. If you wait long enough you may see the white starch settle to the bottom of the glass.

Because dextrin molecules are small, dextrin breaks down into individual dextrin molecules surrounded by water. A solution of dextrin molecules in water is a clear brown color.

The starch and water mixture does not let the light pass through it and so the starch and water mixture has a white cloudy color. The small dextrin molecules form a clear brown solution which light goes through. Starch molecules do not form a solution because they are much bigger than dextrin molecules.

Other things to try

Bread is mostly made of starch. When bread is heated it turns brown on the surface. What do you think the brown substance is?

Young children first starting to eat, or people with trouble digesting starch, eat toast that contains dextrin. When starch or dextrin are digested, they are broken down to individual sugar molecules from which they are made. Dextrin molecules are easier to digest than starch molecules because they are smaller.

26 CAN VINEGAR AND SALT BE USED TO CLEAN COPPER PENNIES?

Materials

Two old, brown pennies   A measuring cup
Vinegar   A teaspoon
Salt   A bowl

Procedure

Pour one-half cup of vinegar into a bowl. Add one teaspoon of salt and stir until all the salt dissolves into the vinegar. Put one of the pennies in the bowl. Wait one minute. Remove the penny from the bowl. Rinse off the penny with water.

BEFORE CLEANING   AFTER CLEANING

Observations

What color is the penny that was placed in the bowl of salt and vinegar? Compare this penny to the other brown penny. Does the penny removed from the bowl look like a shiny, new penny?

Discussion

Older pennies are made of copper. Now pennies are made of zinc in the center and copper on the outside. The copper atoms on the surface of a penny can combine with oxygen in the air. Copper atoms and oxygen molecules can combine to form copper oxide. Copper metal is bright and shiny. Copper oxide is a dull brown color.

When the penny is placed in the salt and vinegar, the copper oxide is removed. Underneath the brown copper oxide is shiny copper metal. It usually takes several years for a brown layer of copper oxide to form on a penny. You can remove this layer in a minute with vinegar and salt.

Vinegar is a mixture of acetic acid and water. When copper oxide is placed in acid, the acetic acid breaks the solid copper oxide apart. The copper in the copper oxide is changed to positive copper ions that become surrounded by water molecules. The oxygen in the copper oxide combines with positively charged hydrogen atoms from the acetic acid to form more water molecules.

Table salt is sodium chloride. Sodium chloride in water breaks into positive sodium ions and negative chlorine ions. These positive and negative ions help the copper oxide to dissolve or break apart in the vinegar.

Other things to try

Get three old, brown pennies and three bowls. Put one-half cup of vinegar in the first bowl. Put one-half cup of water in the second bowl. Put one-half cup of water and two teaspoons of salt in the third bowl. Stir the salt and water until the salt dissolves. Place one penny in each bowl. Wait two minutes and remove each penny. Rinse these pennies with water. Do any of these pennies become shiny? Are salt and vinegar both necessary to clean a penny?

Put one old, brown penny on a plate. Sprinkle salt on the penny until it is covered with a layer of salt. Add a few drops of lemon juice until the salt on top of the penny is wet. Lemon juice contains acid. Wait one minute. Rinse off the penny with water. Is one side of the penny shiny?

27 CAN SOLIDS BE PRODUCED IN SALT WATER WHEN ELECTRICITY IS PASSED THROUGH STEEL NAILS?

Materials

A 6-volt lantern battery

A teaspoon

A measuring cup

Water

Two large steel nails

Salt

A small jar (a baby food jar is a good size)

Two pieces of insulated wire (about ten inches long)

Procedure

ASK AN ADULT TO HELP YOU WITH THIS EXPERIMENT. ELECTRICITY CAN BE DANGEROUS. NEVER PUT HOUSE CURRENT (electricity from a wall outlet) IN WATER. YOU SHOULD ONLY USE A SMALL BATTERY FOR THIS EXPERIMENT. DO NOT LET ANY FLAME GET NEAR YOUR EXPERIMENT.

Fill the measuring cup with one-half cup of water. Add two teaspoons of salt to the water in the measuring cup. Stir until most of the salt has dissolved. Fill the jar with this salt water.

Ask an adult to remove about one-half inch of insulation from both ends of the wires. Connect a wire to the negative (-) terminal of the battery. Wrap the other end of this wire tightly around the top of the first nail. This nail is the negative nail. Connect the second wire to the positive (+) terminal of the battery. Wrap the other end of this wire tightly around the top of the second nail. This nail is the positive nail. Place both nails in the salt water. The nails should be near but not touching each other.

If you see bubbles in the water near the negative nail, you will know the electricity is flowing. If you do not see any bubbles, then you have a loose wire, bad connection, or dead battery. Check the wires and check your battery.

Let the electricity flow for about five minutes. Disconnect the wires from the battery. Remove the nails from the water.

DO NOT LET THE ELECTRICITY FLOW FOR MORE THAN ABOUT FIVE MINUTES SO THAT JUST A SMALL AMOUNT OF GAS IS PRODUCED.

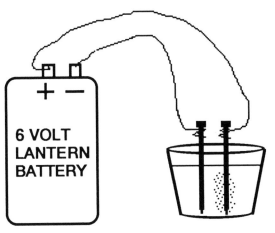

Observations

Is the salt water colorless at the start of your experiment? As you pass electricity through the salt water, does the water change? Does the water change colors? Do you see small solid particles forming and floating in the water?

Discussion

Table salt is sodium chloride. Sodium chloride is made of positive sodium atoms and negative chlorine atoms. When placed in water, salt breaks apart into these positive and negative ions.

At the negative nail, electrons flow into the water. The negative electrons combine with water molecules to produce hydrogen gas and hydroxide ions (OH-).

At the positive nail, metal atoms are changed into positive metal ions and electrons. The electrons flow through the nail and wire back to the positive terminal of the battery. The positive metal ions go into the water.

The positive ions are mostly iron but may also include smaller amounts of manganese, chromium, and nickel that are found in steel. The positive metal ions that go into the water can combine with negative ions such as the hydroxide (OH-) or chloride (Cl-) or hypochlorite (ClO-) that may be present in the water.

The positive and negative ions combine to form small solid particles. A solid formed from ions in solution is referred to as a precipitate. The solid green precipitate formed in this experiment is probably from the combination of iron and hydroxide ions. If the particles formed are very small, they may tend to float in the liquid. If the particles are larger, they will settle to the bottom of the liquid.

Other things to try

Try adding vinegar to a portion of the precipitate solution and see if the solution changes from a green to an orange color. Vinegar is an acid. Try adding baking soda to the orange liquid and see if it will change back to green. Baking soda is a base. The color and arrangement of the solids and ions in solution can change if an acid or base is added to the liquid.

Let the jar sit overnight. Are the precipitate particles large enough to settle to the bottom of the jar?

Repeat this experiment using metal paper clips instead of nails. Do you get the same color changes in the salt water? Does a precipitate form?

Repeat the experiment using vinegar or baking soda instead of salt. Are bubbles produced at the nails? Do any solids form in the salt water?

CAN ELECTRICITY AND COPPER PENNIES TURN WATER BLUE?

Materials

A measuring cup	Baking soda
A 6-volt lantern battery	A spoon
Two new, shiny pennies	Two paper clips
A glass	A small plate

Two pieces of insulated wire (about ten inches long)

Procedure

ASK AN ADULT TO HELP YOU WITH THIS EXPERIMENT. ELECTRICITY CAN BE DANGEROUS. NEVER PUT HOUSE CUR-RENT (electricity from a wall outlet) IN WATER. YOU SHOULD USE ONLY A SMALL BATTERY FOR THIS EXPERIMENT. DO NOT LET ANY FLAME GET NEAR YOUR EXPERIMENT.

Add one-fourth cup of baking soda to a glass. Add one-half cup of water to the glass. Stir for one minute to dissolve as much of the baking soda as possible.

Set the glass on a table and let the undissolved (solid) baking soda settle to the bottom of the glass. Wait five minutes for the baking soda to settle. Carefully pour enough of the liquid from the glass to fill up the plate.

Ask an adult to remove about one-half inch of insulation from the ends of each of the wires. Attach one end of the first wire to the negative (-) terminal on the battery. Attach one end of the second wire to the positive (+) terminal on the battery. Use a paper clip across the top of each penny to attach the free end of each wire to a penny. (If you have wires with alligator clips on them you can attach the wires directly to each penny and not use paper clips.)

Hold the pennies about one-quarter inch apart and place them in the baking soda water covering the plate. Do not let the paper clips or wires touch the water. Hold the pennies in the water for several minutes and watch the water.

If nothing happens then you have a loose wire, bad connection, or a dead battery. Check all the wires.

LET THE ELECTRICITY FLOW THROUGH THE WATER FOR NO MORE THAN FIVE MINUTES.

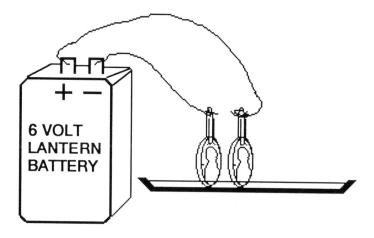

Observations

Do you see bubbles forming around the pennies? Does the water turn a faint blue color near the pennies? Does part of the penny attached to the positive terminal turn blue?

Discussion

A base is a substance that produces a hydroxide ion (OH-) in water. A hydroxide ion is made from a hydrogen atom, an oxygen atom, and an extra electron. Baking soda is a chemical called sodium bicarbonate. Baking soda is a base and produces hydroxide ions when added to water.

At the penny attached to the negative terminal (negative penny), electrons flow into the water. These electrons combine with water to form hydrogen gas and more hydroxide ions. The bubbles formed at the negative penny are hydrogen gas.

At the penny attached to the positive terminal (positive penny), copper atoms leave the surface of the penny and go into the water as positive copper ions. Copper ions in water have a blue color. This blue color is more intense if there are hydroxide ions in the water.

At the positive penny, hydroxide ions combine to form water molecules and oxygen gas. The bubbles formed at the positive penny are oxygen gas.

COPPER IONS ARE POISON. DO NOT PUT THE BLUE WATER IN YOUR MOUTH. POUR THE BLUE LIQUID DOWN THE DRAIN. RINSE THE DRAIN WITH WATER. CLEAN THE PLATE BEFORE USING IT AGAIN.

Other things to try

Repeat this experiment using lemon juice or vinegar. Lemon juice and vinegar are safe household acids. An acid produces a hydrogen ion (H+) in water. Can you get the water to turn blue? Is the color fainter than with the baking soda?

Repeat this experiment with pure water. Does the water turn blue at all? Do you need ions in water for electricity to flow and a chemical reaction to take place?

29 CAN WOOD ASHES CHANGE WATER TO A BASE?

Materials

Red cabbage leaves	Hot water
A measuring cup	A large bowl

Two small jars (baby food jars are a good size.)

Wood ashes (You will need to get wood ashes from an adult who has a fireplace. Enough ashes are needed to cover the bottom of one jar with a layer of ashes about one-half inch deep.)

Procedure

Tear several cabbage leaves into small pieces about the size of a penny. Put one-half cup of cabbage pieces into a bowl. Add two cups of hot water from a sink faucet to the bowl. Wait about ten minutes. The water in the bowl will turn purple. When the water is no longer hot, remove the leaves.

Cover the bottom of one jar with a layer of ashes about the thickness of your finger (less than one-half inch deep). Fill each jar with purple cabbage juice. Watch the jars.

DO NOT GET THE WATER THAT HAS HAD ASHES IN IT ON YOUR SKIN OR IN YOUR EYES. POUR THE WATER DOWN THE DRAIN WHEN FINISHED AND PUT THE ASHES IN THE TRASH.

Observations

Does the water in the jar with no ashes change color? Does the water in the jar with ashes change color?

Discussion

Red cabbage juice contains molecules called <u>indicators</u> that can

RED CABBAGE JUICE IN

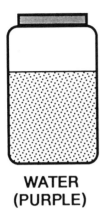 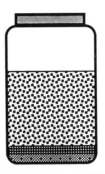

WATER	WATER AND ASHES
(PURPLE)	(BLUE OR GREEN)

be used to identify acids and bases. The indicator molecules in red cabbage are red in acid, blue or green in base, and purple in neutral solutions. Blue indicates a slightly basic solution and green indicates a more basic solution.

A liquid that is not acid or base is said to be neutral. Pure water is neutral. An acid is a substance that produces positive hydrogen ions (H+) which combine with water. A base is a substance that produces hydroxide ions (OH-) in water. A hydroxide ion is made from a hydrogen atom, an oxygen atom, and an extra electron. A water molecule has two hydrogen atoms and one oxygen atom.

Wood is made mostly of molecules containing carbon, oxygen, and hydrogen atoms. When wood is burned most of the carbon, oxygen, and hydrogen atoms in the wood are combined with oxygen molecules in the air to produce carbon dioxide and water molecules. These molecules go into the air and the wood seems to disappear as it burns.

When wood burns, a gray powder called ash is left behind. Ash contains salts and metal oxides that do not burn. The metal oxides are combinations of oxygen atoms with metals such as sodium and potassium.

When metal oxides such as potassium oxide are placed in water, they can combine with water to produce positive metal ions and negative hydroxide ions. These negative hydroxide ions make neutral water change to a base. When the water containing cabbage juice is changed to a base, the color should change from purple to blue or green.

In earlier days, before soap was available in stores, it was made at home. Soap was made by heating grease, water, and a strong base in a pot over a fire. Water was allowed to drip through wood ashes to produce the strong base needed for soap making.

Other things to try

Try adding pieces of wood or sawdust to a jar containing purple cabbage juice. Does this water change to a base? Does the unburned wood contain metal oxides?

HOW MANY FOOD COLORING MOLECULES 30 CAN YOU SEE IN ONE CUP OF WATER?

Materials

Eight tall, clear glasses
Red food coloring
A two-cup measuring cup
A one-cup measuring cup
A piece of white paper

Water
A spoon
Tape
A felt pen

If you do not have eight tall, clear glasses, you can purchase tall, clear plastic glasses in a grocery store.

Procedure

Place a piece of tape on each of the eight glasses. Use the felt pen to label the glasses "1, 2, 3, 4, 5, 6, 7, and 8." Make sure to write on the tape.

Add two drops of red food coloring to a two-cup measuring cup. Fill the two-cup measuring cup with water from a sink faucet. Stir the red-colored water with a spoon. Rinse the spoon with water from the sink faucet.

Now you are going to fill each labeled glass with red-colored water that has been diluted so that each labeled glass has one-half the number of red food coloring molecules in it as the glass before it. Fill the one-cup measuring cup with the red-colored water from the two-cup measuring cup. Pour the red-colored water in the one-cup measuring cup into the glass labeled "1." Rinse the one-cup measuring cup with water from the sink faucet and shake out the excess water.

Add water to the one cup of red-colored water in the two-cup measuring cup until you have two cups of colored water. Stir the colored water with a spoon. Rinse the spoon with water from the sink faucet. Fill the one-cup measuring cup with the red-colored water from

91

the two-cup measuring cup that has been diluted. Pour the one cup of red-colored water in the one-cup measuring cup into the glass labeled "2." The glass labeled "2" now has one-half the number of red food coloring molecules in it as the glass labeled "1."

Repeat the above procedure until each labeled glass is filled. The third time you dilute the red-colored water, place the one cup of red-colored water in the glass labeled "3." The fourth time, add the colored water to the glass labeled "4" and so on. Place the glasses of water on a piece of white paper on a table. Arrange the glasses in order starting on the left with the glass labeled "1" and ending on the right with the glass labeled "8."

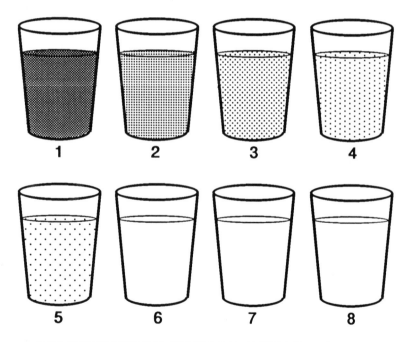

COLORED WATER THAT HAS BEEN DILUTED
UNTIL NO COLOR CAN BE SEEN

Observations

Does the red-colored water become lighter in color each time you dilute the colored water? Which glass no longer has any red color in it?

Discussion

One drop of red food coloring contains approximately one quintillion molecules that give red food coloring its color. One quintillion looks like this when it is written as a number: 1,000,000,000,000,000,000.

In the glass of red-colored water labeled "1" you have this many red food coloring molecules dissolved in one cup of water. One cup of water contains approximately eight septillion water molecules. Eight septillion looks like this when it is written as a number: 8,000,000,000,000,000,000,000,000. There are many more water molecules in the glass labeled "1" than there are red food coloring molecules. In fact, there are eight million (8,000,000) water molecules for every one red food coloring molecule in the glass labeled "1." Although there are more water molecules in the glass labeled "1," there are enough red food coloring molecules in the glass to give the water a red color.

Each labeled glass of water after the glass labeled "1" in the row contains one-half the number of red food coloring molecules as the one before it. For example, the glass of water labeled "2" contains one-half the number of red food coloring molecules that are in the glass labeled "1." The glass of water labeled "3" contains one-half the number of red food coloring molecules that are in the glass labeled "2," and so on. Each labeled glass of water in the row should be lighter in color than the one before it because it contains fewer red food coloring molecules than the one before it.

Eventually the red-colored water becomes so dilute that you can no longer see any red color in the water. Although you can no longer see any red color in the glass of water, there are still many red food coloring molecules in the glass. For example, although you may not see any color in the glass labeled "5," there are still approximately sixty-two and one-half quadrillion (62,500,000,000,000,000) red food coloring molecules in the glass. The reason you may not see any color in the glass labeled "5" is because there are so many more water molecules in the glass than there are red food coloring molecules. In fact, in the glass labeled "5" there are approximately one hundred and twenty-eight million (128,000,000) water molecules for every red food coloring molecule. The red food coloring is too dilute to be seen in the glass of water.

Other things to try

Repeat this experiment with other food colorings. Do you get similar results? Try using green food coloring. Does the colored water become light blue before more dilutions make it colorless? Green food coloring is a mixture of blue and yellow food coloring

Repeat the experiment with ten drops of red food coloring. Does it take more dilutions with water before you no longer see red color in the water?

COMPLETE LIST OF MATERIALS USED IN THESE EXPERIMENTS

Alka-Seltzer tablets

aluminum foil

aluminum pie pan

automobile

Baking soda

balloons

bicycle pump

black shoe polish

blue construction paper

bowls

butter

Carbonated drinks in can

carbonated drinks in glass bottle

carbonated drinks in plastic bottles

chemical lightsticks

clock

coins

cooking oil

cornstarch

Crisco

cups

Dime

dishwashing liquid

drinking glasses

Empty milk jug with lid

Felt pen

flashlight

food coloring

fructose

Gelatin packet, unflavored

grape jelly

ground ginger

Helium-filled balloon

Ice cubes

ice tray

insulated wire

Jars

Lamp

latex paint

laundry detergent

lemon juice

liquid hand soap

Measuring cups

measuring spoons

metal cookie sheet

meter stick

microwave oven

milk

machine oil

Newspaper

Oil based paint

oven

Paper

paper clips

paper towels

pencil with eraser

pennies

pepper

plastic bowl

plastic food wrap

plates

pot holders

Raisins

refrigerator freezer

rubber plumber's plunger

ruler

red cabbage leaves

Salt saucepan

sawdust

scissors

sink

small jars

smooth board

soap

soap bubble liquid and ring

soft drink bottles

spoons

Sprite

steel nails

stove

string

6-volt lantern battery

sugar

sunscreen

Tablespoons

tape

teaspoon

Tide

tire pressure gauge

Vinegar

Watch

water

wax paper

white cloth

wood ashes

Yardstick

yeast

Zip-lock bags

INDEX